SUPERWOMEN
ROLE MODELS

KATE MIDDLETON

Emily Mahoney

PowerKiDS
press

New York

Published in 2017 by The Rosen Publishing Group, Inc.
29 East 21st Street, New York, NY 10010

First Edition

Editor: Katie Kawa
Book Design: Reann Nye

Library of Congress Cataloging-in-Publication Data

Mahoney, Emily Jankowski, author.
 Kate Middleton / Emily Mahoney.
    pages cm. — (Superwoman role models)
 Includes index.
 ISBN 978-1-5081-4834-0 (pbk.)
 ISBN 978-1-5081-4774-9 (6 pack)
 ISBN 978-1-5081-4807-4 (library binding)
 1. Catherine, Duchess of Cambridge, 1982—Juvenile literature. 2. Princesses—Great Britain—Biography—Juvenile literature. 3. Charities—Great Britain—Juvenile literature. I. Title.
 DA591.A45W5558 2016
 941.086'12092—dc23
 [B]
                            2015029392

Manufactured in the United States of America

CPSIA Compliance Information: Batch #BS16PK: For Further Information contact Rosen Publishing, New York, New York at 1-800-237-9932

CONTENTS

THE DUCHESS OF CAMBRIDGE 4

EARLY LIFE 6

THE UNIVERSITY OF ST. ANDREWS 8

LIFE AFTER SCHOOL 10

A ROYAL ENGAGEMENT 12

THE WEDDING OF THE CENTURY 14

LIVING ROYALLY 16

COMMITMENT TO CHARITY 18

CLOSE TO HER HEART 20

HELPING BRITISH CHILDREN 22

CONNECTING WITH PEOPLE 24

A GROWING FAMILY 26

BALANCING WITH GRACE 28

GLOSSARY 31

INDEX 32

WEBSITES 32

THE DUCHESS OF CAMBRIDGE

Many young girls dream of becoming a princess. For Kate Middleton, the life of a princess is her reality! After Kate married Prince William—who's also known as the Duke of Cambridge—in 2011, she became the Duchess of Cambridge and a member of the British royal family.

When many people think of princesses, they think of fancy dresses, castles, and dancing at royal balls. Sometimes Kate gets to dress up in beautiful gowns, but her title means so much more than that. As a member of the royal family, Kate has been able to raise awareness and money for causes that are close to her heart. She's a great role model because she works hard to help those in need, and she does so with kindness and grace.

Kate is also a mother, which is a very hard but very important job!

EARLY LIFE

Kate was born into a family that understands the value of hard work. Catherine Elizabeth Middleton was born on January 9, 1982, in Reading, England. Her mother, Carole, and her father, Michael, met while working as flight attendants. They got married in 1980, and they soon decided to start a family. Kate is their oldest child. She has a younger sister named Philippa (often called Pippa) and a younger brother named James.

After Pippa and James were born, Kate's parents started their own party supply company called Party Pieces, which turned into a multimillion-dollar business. Kate went to a **boarding school** called Marlborough College, where she earned good grades. She also played many sports there, including field hockey.

A WORLD TRAVELER

Even before becoming a member of the royal family, Kate was a world traveler. She used her **gap year** between leaving Marlborough College and starting school at a university to travel. She studied at the British Institute of Florence in Italy. She also volunteered in Chile through a British organization called Raleigh International. The time Kate spent in these countries helped her see the importance of helping people around the world, which she's now able to do as the Duchess of Cambridge.

Kate's parents worked hard to create a successful business. They set a good example for their children.

THE UNIVERSITY OF ST. ANDREWS

Kate started studying at the University of St. Andrews in Scotland in 2001. She graduated in 2005 with a degree in History of Art. Kate met her future husband during her time at this school. They took many classes together and became friends before they began to date. This allowed them to get to know each other long before they were married.

Kate was very active at the University of St. Andrews. She studied for her classes and made many friends. Kate also continued to play sports. She was on the school's field hockey team. Kate also participated in charity events during her time as a student to raise money for different causes.

Kate learned to be independent during her years spent at schools away from home, including the University of St. Andrews, shown here.

LIFE AFTER SCHOOL

After Kate graduated from the University of St. Andrews, she entered the working world. Although she was dating a prince, she continued to work hard, especially at her family's business. She started working for Party Pieces after she finished school. She also worked in London as a **buyer** for a clothing company called Jigsaw Junior.

Kate started her own branch of Party Pieces in 2008. Called First Birthdays, it was a junior brand of its parent company. Kate took on many roles within the family business. She designed catalogues, took photographs, and was involved with the company's marketing. Kate put her interests in design and photography to good use as she worked to help her family's business remain successful.

WILLIAM'S WORK

William began serving his country as a member of the military in 2006. From 2010 to 2013, he worked as a search-and-rescue pilot with the Royal Air Force (RAF). During that time, William was part of 156 search-and-rescue operations, which rescued 149 people. William's years of service—as well as those of others in his family, including his brother, Harry—made Kate especially aware of the importance of helping those who served in England's armed forces.

As the word began to spread about Kate and William's relationship, the media began to follow her around. Kate learned to handle all the cameras, reporters, and fans with grace, which isn't easy!

A ROYAL ENGAGEMENT

On November 16, 2010, Kate and William announced they were engaged to be married. William proposed to Kate while they were on vacation in Kenya. The people of England were very excited because it's not every day a person like them gets to join the royal family!

Kate and William were very happy as well. Although Kate was nervous about joining such a famous family, she also knew she and William would be starting a new life together.

Becoming part of the royal family would also give Kate an opportunity to meet new people and to help charities. She was especially excited to work with children and young adults. Kate planned to use her new royal role to change the lives of people around her for the better.

William proposed to Kate with his late mother's engagement ring.

DIANA, PRINCESS OF WALES

William's mother was Diana, Princess of Wales, who was married to Prince Charles from 1981 to 1996. She died on August 31, 1997, following a car accident in Paris. Diana was known for her work with charities around the world. She was especially involved in helping children's charities and working with people affected by a deadly disease known as AIDS. Diana used her title of princess to raise awareness for many important causes. She set a good example for every princess who will follow her, including Kate.

THE WEDDING OF THE CENTURY

Since so many people in England were excited about their prince getting married, William and Kate's wedding was a huge event. They were married on April 29, 2011. The wedding took place at Westminster Abbey, which has been the official church for all **coronations** and has hosted many royal weddings in England since 1066. Kate gained a husband that day, and she also gained an official title: Her Royal Highness, The Duchess of Cambridge.

After the wedding, Kate and William continued to live on the island of Anglesey in Wales, because Prince William was still part of the RAF at the time. He needed to be close to his base on the island to carry out his duties as a search-and-rescue pilot.

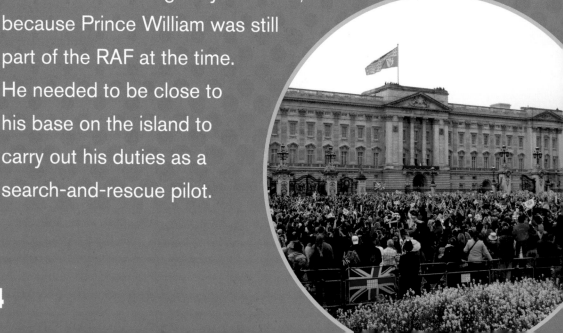

It's been reported that around 24 million people throughout the United Kingdom watched William and Kate's wedding on television. It was also reported that at least 23 million people watched the royal wedding in the United States.

LIVING ROYALLY

Although being a duchess who's newly married to a prince sounds like fun, it also comes with its fair share of responsibilities. These responsibilities include leading ceremonies, meeting with important **dignitaries**, and giving speeches. Kate said giving speeches made her nervous, but she overcame her nerves to do her best in her new role.

William and Kate also travel to other countries on behalf of the royal family. After Kate and William were married, Kate visited countries such as Canada, Malaysia, Singapore, the United States, and New Zealand. She meets with people from each country, and she's often seen meeting with children during these trips. Kate has many fans around the world because of her kindness and grace in such a public role.

William and Kate both love sports, and they travel to watch different sporting events. They were often seen supporting British athletes during the 2012 Summer Olympics in London.

COMMITMENT TO CHARITY

Kate has used her fame and popularity to raise awareness for many important causes and charities. In 2009, William and Harry started their own foundation. Kate formally joined them in this effort in 2011. The Royal Foundation of the Duke and Duchess of Cambridge and Prince Harry focuses on supporting young people and members of the armed forces, as well as conservation efforts.

Kate works closely with the Royal Foundation, which is an important and time-consuming job. She's been able to start projects through the foundation, such as M-PACT Plus. This is a program that helps support children and teenagers whose families are affected by drug and alcohol abuse. The project started in 2013, and Kate's support is one of the main reasons it's been able to help many families.

IN HER WORDS

"Through our foundation we intend to bring a spotlight to bear on some key challenges facing society today at home and abroad, and to lend whatever support we can to those individuals and organizations leading the fight to confront and overcome these challenges."

The Duke and Duchess of Cambridge and Prince Harry

Helping others is very important to William, Kate, and Harry. Their foundation supports many charitable causes in England and around the world.

CLOSE TO HER HEART

Members of the royal family serve as **patrons** for charities and organizations that mean something special to them. Once Kate married William, she began to choose which charities she would support as a royal patron. She chose to support charities that reflected what matters most to her.

Kate's love for art can be seen in her support of the National Portrait Gallery. Her love for sports is reflected in her choice to be a patron for an organization called SportsAid. This charity aims to raise money to support young people in Britain who want to compete in the Olympic Games or **Paralympic Games**. Kate is also a patron and volunteer for the Scout Association, which helps young people learn life skills through outdoor activities.

IN HER WORDS

"I really hope I can make a difference, even in the smallest way. I am looking forward to helping as much as I can."
Interview with Tom Bradby of ITV News, given in November 2010

Kate is shown here supporting British athletes at the 2012 Paralympic Games in London. Through her support of SportsAid, she's been able to help young people who want to compete in the Paralympic Games.

HELPING BRITISH CHILDREN

Many of the charities Kate supports as a patron are focused on helping young people. One charity close to Kate's heart is the East Anglia Children's Hospices (EACH). This organization helps children with life-threatening illnesses and their families. Its goal is to care for sick children and those who love them in whatever way it can, especially at the end of a sick child's life.

Kate also supports an organization called Place2Be, which is focused on children's mental health concerns. Place2Be works out of British schools to help children receive the mental health care they need.

Kate's charity work provides a great example of giving back to others. She uses her fame and title to raise not just money, but also awareness for organizations she believes in.

IN HER WORDS

"While I am new to this field, and have much to learn, I strongly believe that the issue of mental health problems for young people has to be tackled. Too many young people are suffering from emotional problems, and the impact can be simply devastating."

Letter written in Place2Be's *The Journal* in 2013

When Kate travels to other counties, she often visits schools to meet with young people. This photograph was taken during her 2014 visit to a school in Australia.

23

CONNECTING WITH PEOPLE

William's mother, Diana, is remembered as "The People's Princess" because of her popularity with people in England and around the world. Kate is following in her footsteps. She's spent a lot of time visiting with the people of her country. She's often seen spending time with children, and her support for children's charities is an important part of her work as a member of the royal family.

Kate didn't grow up in a famous family. She went to school, and she worked for her family's business. Her roots as a normal girl have made her very popular with people in England and around the world. She's set a good example for how to stay true to yourself and what you believe in when your life changes in a major way.

IN HER WORDS

"The challenges facing children in today's society can seem overwhelming…. Providing support for these vulnerable children, and their families, by caring for their mental health and emotional wellbeing is key."

Letter written in Place2Be's
***The Journal* in 2013**

This photograph shows Kate visiting a school in England to see the work done through The Art Room, which she supports as a patron. The Art Room is a charity that teaches children to use art as a way to deal with emotional and mental difficulties.

A GROWING FAMILY

In addition to being an **activist** and a duchess, Kate is also a mother. Kate and William have two children: George Alexander Louis and Charlotte Elizabeth Diana. George was born on July 22, 2013, and Charlotte was born on May 2, 2015. George is third in line to **inherit** the throne, while Charlotte is fourth. Many people were excited for the new royals to be born. People even waited outside the hospital where Kate gave birth to see the babies for the first time.

Kate enjoys being a mother, and her children are very important to her. While it can be difficult to raise royal children, Kate and William want to be very involved in their childrens' lives.

A NEW SET OF RULES

Before 2013, if William and Kate had another son after Charlotte, he would have gone ahead of her in line to inherit the throne. However, the Succession to the Crown Act of 2013 made it so a younger son can't take the place of an older daughter in the **line of succession**. This was a very important change. It showed that women are just as worthy as men to inherit the throne in England.

Kate has now taken on another important role in the royal family—mother to George and Charlotte.

BALANCING WITH GRACE

From Duchess of Cambridge and wife of the future king of England, to charitable patron and mother—Kate Middleton has many titles. She's a great role model because she's very committed to everything she does, and she's helpful in her community and around the world. She also works hard to be a good mother to her two young children. It's difficult to balance so many titles, but Kate does it gracefully.

What truly makes Kate special is that she helps those who aren't as fortunate as she is. She works hard to help others, which is something that anyone—royal or not—should try to do in their life.

IN HER WORDS

"I think the people around home are very supportive to us…. And I think if they feel you are doing the right thing, you can only be true to yourself, and you sort of have to ignore a lot of what's said—obviously take it on board—but you have to be yourself."

Interview with Tom Bradby of ITV News, given in November 2010

Kate uses her fame and influence for good. That makes her a great role model not just for girls, but for people everywhere.

TIMELINE

- **January 9, 1982:** Kate is born in Reading, England.
- **2001:** Kate begins college at the University of St. Andrews in Scotland, where she meets Prince William.
- **2005:** Kate graduates with her degree in History of Art.
- **November 16, 2010:** Kate and William announce their engagement.
- **2011:** Kate officially lends her support to William and Harry's foundation, which becomes known as the Royal Foundation of the Duke and Duchess of Cambridge and Prince Harry.
- **April 29, 2011:** Kate and William are married at Westminster Abbey.
- **2013:** Kate launches M-PACT Plus.
- **July 22, 2013:** Kate gives birth to her son, George.
- **May 2, 2015:** Kate gives birth to her daughter, Charlotte.

GLOSSARY

activist: Someone who acts strongly in support of or against an issue or cause.

boarding school: A school at which most of the students live during the school year.

buyer: A person whose job is to purchase things for a large business, especially a retail store.

coronation: A ceremony in which a crown is placed on the head of a new king or queen.

dignitary: A person who has a high rank or important position.

gap year: A year a person spends traveling or working before continuing their studies.

inherit: To get something such as a title after a person in your family dies.

line of succession: The order in which a person gets a title after the person who had that title before has died.

Paralympic Games: A series of international sporting contests for athletes with disabilities.

patron: An important person who uses their wealth or influence to help a cause.

INDEX

A
Art Room, The, 25

C
charities, 8, 12, 13, 18, 20, 22, 24, 25, 28
Charlotte, 26, 27, 30
children, 7, 12, 13, 16, 18, 22, 24, 25, 26, 28

E
East Anglia Children's Hospices, 22
engagement, 12, 30

F
First Birthdays, 10

G
George, 26, 27, 30

J
Jigsaw Junior, 10

M
Marlborough College, 6
mother, 5, 6, 12, 13, 24, 26, 27, 28
M-PACT Plus, 18, 30

P
parents, 6, 7
Party Pieces, 6, 10
patron, 20, 22, 25, 28
Place2Be, 22, 24
Prince Harry, 10, 18, 19
princess, 4, 13, 24
Prince William, 4, 10, 11, 12, 13, 14, 15, 16, 17, 18, 19, 20, 24, 26, 30

R
RAF, 10, 14
royal family, 4, 6, 12, 16, 20, 24, 27
Royal Foundation of the Duke and Duchess of Cambridge and Prince Harry, 18, 19, 30

S
Scout Association, 20
sports, 6, 8, 17, 20
SportsAid, 20, 21

U
University of St. Andrews, 8, 9, 10, 30

W
wedding, 14, 15

WEBSITES

Due to the changing nature of Internet links, PowerKids Press has developed an online list of websites related to the subject of this book. This site is updated regularly. Please use this link to access the list: www.powerkidslinks.com/sprwmn/kmid